The Breeze of
Love and Life

The Breeze of Love and Life

PERUMAL MUTHUKUMAR

PARTRIDGE
A Penguin Random House Company

To order additional copies of this book, contact
Partridge India
000 800 10062 62
orders.india@partridgepublishing.com

www.partridgepublishing.com/india

DEDICATION

I take pride in
Dedicating this work
To all the Thinkers of the world who
altered the course of our thinking....

Michael Dobbs,
Rossgarrow. Milford, County Donegal,
Ireland

A LETTER FROM THE FAMILY OF EYRE BURTON POWELL*

The first Principal of presidency College, Chennai.

My family are Anglo Irish and for many generations had worked in India and were very fond of India.

I met Professor Muthukumar when I was on holiday in November 2013 in Chennai with my wife Corinne. We were visiting Presidency College in Chennai where there is a very fine statue of my great grandfather Eyre Burton Powell (my mother's grandfather).

*Professor Powell graduated as Wrangler (top of his year in Mathematics) from Cambridge University in 1840. He arrived in Chennai 1848 to take charge of a new school. He was the first Principal of Presidency College and was Director of Public Education in Chennai from 1862 to 1875. He is referred to in Wikepdia as "a legendary British educationist" and his legacy is "pioneering Western education in Madras" (now Chennai). His protégés include C.V.Runganada Sastri, Sir A.Sashayya Sastrie, Sir T. Madhava Rao, and V.Ramiengar.

My mother was very proud of the work of her grandfather in the College as are members of my generation.

Professor Muthukumar very kindly showed us the various reminders of the work of my great grandfather including the main Assembly Hall of the College named "Powell Hall" after him. He also introduced us to the Principal and Bursar of the College.

I am therefore very glad to have the opportunity to write a word of appreciation to this volume of Poetry. I have enjoyed reading it, and admire his sensitive and imaginative use of the English Language, and his insight into some of the problems of our human existence.

I hope that other readers of these poems will enjoy reading them as much as I have.

Michael Dobbs,
Rossgarrow. Milford, County Donegal, Ireland

Michael Dobbs was a British Naval Officer and English Solicitor and was a great grandson of Eyre Burton Powell, who was the first Principal of The Presidency College Chennai and then The Director of Public Education, Madras Presidency during British India.

THE STREAM OF LOVE

LOVE

Deep into my eyes
you stay.
My wet eyes
with your
moistured thoughts
refuse to blink
for it might
hurt **you.**

KISS...

May be kiss is an
attempt to align the
strong currents of love.

May be an attempt to
understand the tides of love.

May be an attempt
of lips
to understand the heart.

EYES

The Eloquence of
Your eyes......
---The only available
Literature of love.
Dear
Thanks for
Enveloping my
Life in your love
With the
Eloquence of your eyes...

MIND IN FLOOD

Have you ever
seen mind
in flood.
Dear
You can
See the mind of mine
flowing with the
raging thoughts of
you.

You can
See the mind of mine
flooded with the thoughts of
you.

DAY AND NIGHT

Day and night are neighbours
they do not meet
They merge on each other
like the longing lovers
while they meet....

THE WEATHER OF LOVE

The weather of wind is hot
while crossing a desert
The weather of wind is cold
while crossing the Himalayas...
Weather changes
But wind exists...

So are love and life...
Even life goes through
changes like the wind...
Dear
In a life that keeps changing
Love alone lives with no change...

MY 'SELF'

The road towards my 'self' is
Smooth, safe and serene...
The road is not less travelled
It was travelled by many great friends of mine
Who are great to my heart still ...
The road towards my 'self' is full of
Heavenly flowers and divinely fragrance...
The road may lead you
to the destination of my 'self'...
And interestingly... my dear...
My 'self' has no destinations...
It has way for life!
It has way for love!
It has way for happiness!
And, It has way for heavenliness!
Glad I am for your Journey
Towards me...
Dear
I see in you
'Myself'
on your arrival....

SEED AND SOIL

Seed and soil are the
Silent partners of love...
Their commitment to each other
is found in their
exercise of germination.
and
Their love for each other
is found in soil
Strengthening the seed to
Grow down as 'roots'
And Grow up as 'trees'...

The deeper they travel
The stronger their freedom of love is...
As the tree grows to
Symbolize the Love of the seed and soil...
It also grows to live
for the life of love on the Earth...
Dear listen
The tree lives to preserve
the love of seed and soil
to reserve life on this beautiful planet
The Earth...

Alas...
No one on this beautiful Earth
Knows the strength of this beautiful love...
And
No one on this Earth knows the seed and soil as the
Silent partners of love...
Dear
It is in this commitment to each other
The seed of life and love grows.

FEELINGS

Day is a visitor of dusk
And
Night is a visitor of dawn
They meet and depart everyday
With grace....
They do not bid farewell
But they fair well to reach
Each other in their relationship...
as and when
they meet and part...
So are feelings and emotions...
Feelings and emotions are
The wise visitors of mind and heart
They too meet and depart in grace...
They do not bid farewell
But they fair well
to reach each other in relationship...
And make memories memorable...

YOU AND ME

World is after
the attractions
of opposite sex.

YES
You and me
are no way
different from
this nature.

YES
we are no way
different from
this magnetism

YES
we are no way
different from
this symbiotic synthesis
of this **S**pecial **L**ove.

NUANCES OF LOVE

Love
remains a
Teacher for Teaching
the compassion of
Love in
infinite measures.
Hence
I worship
My love
for teaching me
the nuances of a musician
while
composing the compassion of love...

CONFESSION

I see
in your eyes
the confession
of a cosmic Love.

I see
in your voice
the commands of
Royal descendents.

I see
in your smile
the essence of Divinity.

I see in you now
the confluence of
Cosmic Royal Divinity
radiating the
charm of enviable Love.

LIGHT OF LOVE

The sun and the moon
never meet
but they share
light for their life.

You and me
hardly meet
but
remain a
light of our life
by the
light of our love.

SEED OF LOVE

The seed
of love
I sow,
gets carried
along the winds
like the seeds of cotton
and
gets rooted into the soil
and
gets sprouted again
as seeds of love
elsewhere and everywhere.

Is it not
my duty to liberate
the World
with the seeds
of my love?

YOUR ARRIVAL

Dear
All changes
in my life appeared as
Challenges
before your arrival...
And
All challenges
in my life
has become changes
on your arrival...!

FREEDOM

Freedom is not
the liberation
of one 'self'
But the
Freedom of
Other 'self'
Dear
I started
Loving a life
From
Living a life
Since the sanctions
Of your selfless love...

ATTRACTION

As we are
Attracted to each other
We are also
Addicted to each other
We are
Attracted in life
And
addicted in love

May be the
Spice of happiness
We relish
Are churned
out of this simple Addiction...

WORK

The only work
I do now is
thinking...!
And
The only
Thinking I do
is
Thinking of you...!

FEELINGS

I feel like saying
Something to you
And
I have something
To say about my
Feelings
May be I am
Stranded in search of
Words to say something
about my feelings
May be there is no
Saying
only feeling
Exists in love...

DREAM

If dream is unreal
living for it
is real...
So are
Love and Life...
If love is unreal
living for it
is real...

DAY AND NIGHT

The day ends with the
Note of life...
And
The night ends with the
Note of love...
Dear Listen
In a life
of a romantic love
there is no end
There is only beginning....

MISSING LOVE

I am not destined to
Miss my missing love
for long
hence
I am inclined to
fetch my missing love
even from
far of destination.
It is not the question of
What I miss
It is the question of
What I don't want to miss...
...in love...

DISTURBANCES

Rare to see the
Sun and moon meet
And
When they meet
They meet on eclipse day
And
When they meet
They are so disturbed
And
They distract so many
as spectators...
So are lovers
Like eclipse they meet
And
When they meet...
They meet
With
Disturbances and distractions
...For not of their own fault...

PERFECTION

My life is
Full of your love
And
My love is
Full of your life...
Dear
Only in our love and life
I trace the
Equations of perfect balance...

FOR YOU….. FOR EVER

My Life for You
may not
compensate your
memorable past
but may
console your present
by my future declared
for you......forever.

DREAMS

Night is not beautiful
For its blanket of silence..
Night is not beautiful
For the silence it owns...
Night is not beautiful
For the darkness it owns
Dear
Night is actually beautiful
for witnessing the
dreams of your love...
While
I am fast asleep.....!

CELIBACY

Ecstasy of my poetic celibacy
gets renounced
When your *smile*
Collides with the lashes
of my eyes....

FEELINGS

Neither
Could I live with you
Nor
Would I live without you
Dear
I am with the
Flooded feelings
Wedded to me...
How uncertain are
the offers of happiness...!

It appears to be mine.
But
Not of mine.
Dear
I see here a cloud of sadness
in the appearances of happiness.........

AUTOCRAT

Thoughts of you are
Disturbing me
Distracting me
And
Destroying the
other thoughts of mine
living
other than you....
So *autocrat* you are
in reigning the
Entices of my romance..

INSPIRATION

I may not be of your
Inspiration always....
But
I can be of your
Respiration always....
My Love
Be my Life...

MOTHER AND CHILD

Apart from each other
The mother and child....after delivery....
Apart they are
Away they are
And not away
from each other
in their Love......
The life of love is so similar like this.......
Apart they are
Away they are
And not
Away from each other
in their love....
Dear
This is the essence of love....
Greatness of love can be achieved
Only with the goodness of life....

APPEARANCE

There are many who admire the
Appearance of the Himalayas
There are not many who would
Admire the eternity of the Himalayas...
Similarly
There are many who would admire
The appearance of love
And
There are not many who would admire
The Eternity of Love
Dear
I admire the
Eternity of your Love
And
Not the appearance of your love alone...

THE LANE OF HAPPINESS

Between the breath
of mine lives
the memory of
Yours......
And
Between the beat
of my heart stays
the thought of
Yours......
Between the lane of my
Love and life lies the
Past
Present
And the
Future of my happiness ....

DEAR MOM

You deserve the
best of things in this world...
My only regret is
I could offer only
what is humanely possible
And not
Divinely possible....

SILENCE

In silence the flow
of my breath
In silence the glow
of my feelings
In silence the
Aroma of my life
And
In silence
exist the
Armour of my love.........

LISTEN

My dear
sweet dream
listen......!
If
Miss-understanding
is love
then
I wish to live in an understanding
with the **Miss** I miss..
....all my life....

EXISTENCE

A seed grows
And it is invisible in its
Existence and experiments...
A seed grows
And it grows to say
It's fertile to unleash happiness
Similarly
Love grows and it
grows to say it's fertile
to unleash happiness in life....
Dear
Like seed even love is
invisible in its
Existence and in its Experiments...

FLOW OF LOVE

Amidst sleeplessness
I trace my sleepless love...
Amidst hopelessness
I trace the hope of my love...
Amidst numbness
I trace the feelings of my love..
Even amidst lifeless emotions
I trace the life of love...
Dear
Thanks for being the udder of my life
where I see the flow of love
instantly and incessantly....

FRAGILE FEELINGS

I am not resting in you
I am actually nesting in you...
Dear
Any distraction is a disturbance
for a Nesting Bird......
So are my feelings...
My feelings for you are
Nesting in you... and not Resting in you...
Hence
Any distraction is a disturbance...
My feelings are
So fragile
And
So insecured
like the heart of a little
Nesting bird....
Dear
Nest of mine is
Resting in you....
Care me and carry me says
'The feelings'
living for you..

THE STREAM OF LIFE

EMERALD VALLEY

So beautiful the valley is...
I see young leaves adorning
the old roots
I see young flowers adorning
the old leaves
I see the formation of clouds
adorning the long ranges
I see pregnant clouds
appearing and disappearing into the forest

I see this pregnant clouds delivering
drizzles while crossing me
I see this drizzles dressing
my flight of happiness
day and night...
I even see young animals honouring the valley
with the birth of their young ones amidst
the sizzling stream of the valley...

I see in me a wish
Wishing me to own this nature...

'Knowing well'
the impossibility of owning
and still
trying to own this bounty nature
is imprinting in me the
signature of sadness...

So beautiful the valley is...
for imparting the
Sequences of happiness
and the
Signature of sadness
in equal measures...
For missing something
Not to be missed...:!

(This valley is located in Ooty of South India and it
was written during my stay there for a week)

CLONNING OUR MIND FOR A GREATER CAUSE...

Let us clone our minds to build
a great nation.
Let us build a better destiny
for many younger generations born
unknown to themselves about
the cause of their birth.
Let us be an umbilical cord
for those unborn and just born souls.
Let us carve the fate of their
destiny by our decision at this moment.
Let us design our destination amidst
the roaring waves of social and family commitments.
Let us mould our mind and liberate
the society from the clutches of conventions
and customs by clubbing our minds together.
Let us relieve the ill society, the social pain
it is carrying, for ages...

Let the vibrations of our breath
pulsate the heart of
the society by the service
of our
heart and mind.

MOTHER

The sound of my breath
the music of my heart beat
and
the rhythm of my nerves
are the royal symphony
orchestrated since my birth.

I was
detached from the warmth
of my mothers womb
breaking the silence of my
conceived attachment
to unfold the
'silence of silence'
-the spring of my
mothers love.

REVOLUTION

Surprised.....I am...!
by the convulsions of
social revolution
being sedated
by the senseless leaders
across the nation,
conveniently convincing
the
caste and communal card
in the minds of blazing public
for prowling in
pride with power.

A TEACHER

Feared learning
for the fear of teachers.
Loved teaching
for the love for teachers.

A
Memorable childhood reminiscence
that
revolved my schooling
evolved my teaching
and
resolved my living as a Teacher...

A POET

Neither a day
Nor an event
but the
intricacies of life
initiated me
into the realms
of poetic ecstacy.

May be the
tides of
pain and passion in life
Smeared me
had
reared me
with the columns
of poems.

SEX

Sex is a State of
yogic bliss.

A resourceful recreation
which begins with the
discovery of a yogic stretch.

A game of umpires exploring
emotive pleasures in
a secluded stadium.

It is a fusion of
perspiration and respiration.
...a tiring process for
a retiring nucleus
to the respective conceivement base
to generate a generation.

A WOMAN SPEAKS...

Sculpting the flesh of man
in the womb of mine...
Scripting the happiness of him
in the mind of mine...
Sketching the life of him
along the life of mine...
So engrossed in
Sculpting
Sketching and
Scripting in silence his happiness...
So engrossed in imparting duties
With no endorsement on my rights...

The life of women
Continues
as a duty
with
Forsaken rights...

AS I AM

No one would admire you so much
As I am
No one would adore you so much
As I am
No one would reign you so much
As I am
No one would love you so much
As I am
My love
No one would be so autocrat in
Owning the pride of
Owning you...so much
As I am...

My love
Be mine
Until
My breath fades...

LOVE

The showers of mothers love
is inadequate for a child
even after it reaches adulthood...
My dear
I live inside the
Motherhood of your love
Hence the showers of your love
remains inadequate always
eventhough
I moved
from infant to adult in
the passage of my love for you...

MEN AND WOMEN

Men and women are
Conceived as socialist and
delivered as
Capitalist...
Men and women are
born as socialist
and live as
Capitalist...
Infants ability to socialise
mostly are mistaken for a Socialist
And
Adults inability to socialise
mostly are mistaken for a Capitalist...

In conflict the world of mind
And
In contradictions the world of life....

GRASS

A lone grass is beautiful
But
A grass in group is attractive...
The unity of grass
Displays the strength of
Beauty and attraction...
A lone grass attracts destruction
And
A grass in group attracts attention...
Dear
Existing is beautiful
But
Existing in style is attraction...

Do you know something?
A life of grass
is the
Lesson of our life...

MEMORY OF LOVE

Memory of life
may be smart
but not smarter than
the smartness
of love...
The difference is
Life imparts events
And
Love imparts memories...
Dear
Remember something...
Events are delible
but
Memories are indelible...
The memory of love
lasts until the
Memory of life fades...

CASTE CONFLICT

....an untiring warfare
of Centuries
sustained for the
sustenance of hierarchy
by few
glossy caste groups
straining and staining
the Human Welfare
by fueling
the Human Warfare.

MARINA BEACH

Beneath the sea
And
Beyond the sky
are our thoughts
while teasing
your tides on
your shores.

Amazing to see
your tireless performance
while
absorbing the
joys and aches
of your
visitors
beyond the barriers
of race, religion and sex.

You are the living
legend of the Earth.

You are uniting the
Bonds of the beings
and
blending their emotions
tirelessly
tide after tide
for ages.

VOICE OF A TREE

I stand for you
All my life

I live for you
All my life

I care for you
All my life

Despite my love for you
All my life,
You are contesting me
All your life.

Have mercy
Have mercy for your life.

Save me
And
SAVE YOUR LIFE.

A DEDICATION TO MY FATHER

In his
Supreme sacrifice
I stand.

In the
Experiments
Of his life
I sustain.

In the
Philosophy of his
Love
I survive.

FOREST

I was not
Certain about
My interest
For you
So
I had not
Ascertained
My rights
On you

Hence I
Lost You
And
Lost myself.

DEFORESTATION

When everything
seemed to be mine
I had taken it
for granted.

when everything was
losing ground
I wanted everything
around.

what I left
was lost
and
what I lost
has left.

ON HUMAN BONDAGE

Let us feed the Earth
the strength
to live and to lead
millions for millions
of years.

Let us show the world
the bonds of love
and
the bonds of friendship.

Let us realize the
World being drenched
with poverty, hunger,
disease and death.

Let us be concerned for
the World of
Suffering human feelings.

Let us be concerned of
the paradox of
this present.

CONVERSATION

May be
you are the owner
But I am the partner
Of the languages
Your EYES
Converse with.

CHILDHOOD ON THE ROADSIDE

What a life they live!
What a life they lead!

Along gutters their childhood
Along the drainage their playmates

What a paradox!
On the oneside
life on Rolls-Royce

On the otherside
life on roadside
uncared
unhygienic
moments of childhood
on the roadside.

INDEPENDENCE DAY

Celebrations of Independence Day
With pomp and show.
Independence Day with
Nationalistic fervour
every year.

Where is my food
Where is my Childhood
Where is my independence
cries a child
on the road side
every day........!

POOR

A
Class of
Denominations
Dominated by
Various other classes.

A
Class always
Misused and misplaced.

A
Class always left to
live with the
Miscarried justice...

REMINISCENCE

Years ago
On the banks of
this great river
the reminiscence of
My childhood began.

Years after
on the same banks
of this great river,
along the flow of the streams...
The childhood of my
Child begins...

Along the
Wings of change...
and
Along the
Winds of change
Flows quietly the
Reminiscence of this great river...

LOVE

With scrambles
a family lives
on the pavement

Along with them
a dog
who shares their meal.

How fortunate is
the dog for being with the people
of *love, care* and *concern.*

METRO LIFE

Vast a city
Fast a life.

Hardly any time
For
friends and family.

Hours spent on
Commuting and competing.

A socialist
In the train
While sharing
The space with
Vendors and beggars.

A philanthropist
While disbursing alms
to the beggars.

A capitalist
while
commenting and
condemning
the
streets and street dwellers.

Vast a city
Fast a life.

A City Life
filled and fuelled
with
Idealogues.

PRAYERS

Year after year
the festivals of
Religions
Day after day
the prayers and demands
communicated to
the surprise of
Gods and Godesses.

Moments after moments
the
demands and needs laid to
the
Gods of young, and ageless
Religions.
In puzzle the
Lords of Beliefs.

ON JUVENILE POVERTY

Roofless and Rootless
their life on roadside...
I see their eyes
floating in tears

I see tears
floating in their life

I see hunger and poverty
as their constant companion
I see their feelings
stricken in silence...
I see those young life being
abused seduced and reduced
into ashes...
A betrayal of nations hope...
Sad to see a nation
sleeping on this dormant
volcanic silence...

NATURE

World over travels the cloud
as a citizen of sky...

The cloud
while on a journey
Date with thunder and
flirt with lightning
And showers as rain...

Awaits all life on earth...
The mating of cloud
With thunder and lightning
For the showers of rain...

World over people
Wait for the arrival of this
Pregnant cloud
to deliver the rain of life...
for the life on earth...

SOMETHING

For want of something
was born desires
For want of something
was born leaders
For want of something
was born dictators
For want of something
was born saints
For want of something
was born prophets
For want of something
was born lovers
For want of something
was born the
Feelings for each other
And
For want of this
Missing life
The world exists...

BEAUTY

Rainbow is beautiful
But
disappears after a while
Cloud is beautiful
But disappears after rain
Dew is beautiful on grass
But
disappears on seeing sun
on every morning...
Even the sun and the moon
disappear and appear
again and again....
Dear
What ever has disappeared will reappear
is the 'law of nature'
'Nothing ends and everything begins'
How beautiful it is...
To see 'Nature'
as a Teacher of Continuity...

HAPPINESS

Honey
So industrious your eyes are...!
Your eyes are so industrious like
the Honey bee of a Honey comb
while collecting the
Nectar of Happiness...
And
My dear
Believe me
your eyes are
so industrious
And
So illustrious
in giving me the
Honey of Happiness...

PATHOS OF STREET CHILDREN

Left alone on the streets
With
the taste of tears
And with the
Taste of sadness...
A beautiful painting
Desecrated by parents
And
Destroyed by society...
Like a fallen kite towards
Unknown destinations... a life...
A uniformity of a unkind gestures
Towards this growing young pals...
Sad to see the birth of this innocence
Being pressed into the passage of ignorance...
Sad to see the
Nation of glory
And
People of wisdom
leaving aloof the
Street children to
Taste the tears of sadness
ALONE ALWAYS...

VOYAGER

Unlike the Seafarer
Only the Voyager of great seas
Knows
the Depth of Sea
And
The Strength of sea...
Similarly
Only the Voyager of great strength
Knows that the
Depth of sea is the
Strength of sea...
So is the voyage of love...
Only the Voyager of true love
Knows really the
Depth of love
as the
Strength of love...
Dear
Only the depth of love could
Display and Disclose the
Strength of life...

LIFE

The pond is still...
The sun is scorching
and still stays smiling....the lotus
The lotus blossoms and brittles
only in such scorching sunlight
The scorching sun infact
makes the beauty of lotus visible...
Similarly
It is the pain that makes us
visible and
It is the pain and sufferings
that visit us makes us
blossom and brittle like lotus...
Lotus is wise
while
meeting the scorching sun.
Dear
We shall be wise like the
lotus of a little pond...
We shall also blossom and brittle
with the beauty of compassion
amidst the odds of our life...

ON THE DEATH OF A RIVER-COUUM

The river is dead..
A river once was
passing through the
city is now a dead river....
Through the city...
No no...
Throughout the city the
river travels with acute stench...

A river was killed and allowed to
decompose into a drainage of the whole city....
On the banks of this
dead river
colonies of life.....
As labourers
As migrant workers
And
Sometime as a true citizens
during the election festival....
Sad to see
Children
Vendors

And
Criminals sharing
the banks of the
river equally for their games...
Sad to see our nation
being saddled on the seat of democracy
with the principle of socialism.....
So mute we are in this nation as
citizens of democracy....
So futile our fertile
existence to Co-exist
amidst this stench of pain....

Cooum is a river that runs through Chennai city in
Tamilnadu, India

MAJESTIC PREVALENCE

It was pitch dark.
And there was a light.
Vow..!
How beautiful the light was !
So beautiful it was
while
dispelling the beauty of darkness.
So happy I was
while
the light was litting my happiness.
So gentle the darkness was
while
letting the light to take over
 its majestic prevalence.
So beautiful the feeling was
and
it lasted until I realised
the light I saw was only
of a *melting candle*..
Never had I felt the regret
of loosing the last light..
until....
I had the warmth of my love
holding the light of my life..
.....closer to my heart....

THE BREATH

I am observing my breath closely
and
it travels very closely and continuously
with me and within me.
My breath has liberty
to travel away and go away from me ..
and it's not going away..
I see my breath attending to me
and as well very attentive to my
pain and pleasure..
The journey of my breath
enjoys the warmth of mine
hence
I enjoy the rhythm of its love. ..
So mutual
the love of mine for my breath
and the breath of mine for me....
We do not take chance
in sharing the warmth for each other..
We know very well that
in our love for each other we exist...

Dear
We also know that
We exist in life
Until
We exist in love..
So wonderful are the
Journey of me and my breath
and
So similar are the journey of
My Life and My Love....

EPITAPH

There may be a last
Visitor beside us before
Our last breath......
Either it could be
True love
or the
Truth of love...
Dear
The last visitor
before the
last visit of
our breath could be
Either
You or Me.....
May be
It is not the time to say
But
It is the time to register
the true love
in the hours of **TRUTH**...

JOURNEY

The light of sun travels
Unmindful towards
unknown destinations..
In its journey stumbles upon
Heavenly bodies.... The planets...
In its journey towards the Earth
meets the people
And
Remains disturbed by
Seeing the warm earth
becoming hotter and hotter
day by day
By earthly people's
Insane inventions - **THE POLLUTION**

A DAY

A day is enough
A day is enough for my life
A day is enough to feel my
Life and death
A day is enough for my happiness
A day is enough for my sorrows
A day is enough to know myself
A day is enough to know others
A day is enough to give my best
A day is enough to know my
Destiny and destinations..
A day is enough to travel to all the
Destinations of my feelings...
A day is enough to give the
Best of my fragrance to all...
A day is enough to learn the art of happiness...
Be Happy and learn the art of happiness....
Says a**.... FRAGRANT FLOWER...**

... DEAR

Dreams are not the
destination of love
but the
designation of love...
Where
Something becomes everything
And
Everything becomes something.

SEA OF CHANGE

I could not see the eyes
I had seen earlier
I could not see the smile
I had seen earlier
I could not hear the voice
I heard earlier
I could not enjoy the life
I had enjoyed earlier
I could not feel the love
I felt earlier
I could not enjoy the childhood
I enjoyed earlier
I see here a sea of change from
Childhood to adulthood
I see a sea of change from the
Past to the present...
May be change in life is
Inevitable...
And it is also inevitable to live on it..

MIND

Like the wings of the
winter birds
disappearing into the
foggy weather
'**YOU**' keep
disappearing into the memories
of the past and the dreams of
the future.
Tirelessly like the full moon tide
raging the thoughts with
the past and future...
While I`m
fasting for your present
'**YOU**' are feasting with
the past and future.
Come on !
My Dear
My Love
Dissolve into My `Self '
and
retire to the World of Present
Let us flock together to
The World of Liberation - The World of Happiness....

EXPERIENCE WITH THE TRUTH

Sweep and **M**arch into ***Vipassana****
is a journey into
the sounds of silence (mind)
and
the silence of sounds (matter)
with the realization
of truth
-the genesis of
love and compassion.

*Vipassana is an ancient technique of meditation taught by Buddha and it's the experience of the author in this meditation.

On the question of independence for India

Winston Churchill said ...

> ....the Hindus will seek to drive out the Muslims ...*

> profiteering and corruption will flourish....
> Indian millionaires grow rich on sweated labour, richer will become more powerful and even richer....

In the opinion of the House, the last 50 years proved Churchill Right.

IS THE OLD IMPERIALIST RIGHT AFTER ALL?

Fraternity of Fundamentalism
gave birth to twins.
They are Hindu India
and Muslim Pakistan.

Independence ensured insurance
of insecurity because
independent era of India
is the golden age for the illegal
`customer of comforts' -the corrupts.

These illegal off springs are
legitimised by the
`blinkered' bureaucrats.

This seductive nation is being
seduced by the `sensitive patriots'
-the politicians.

Leaders of the past fought for
our independence.
Leaders of the present are fighting
for their inter-dependence
to soak the citizens
in dependence.

Yes Mr. Churchill
there is a subtler
truth in your statement.

But, Mr.Churchill
why should `you' shed
crocodile tears
for our problems.

We wish to face our crisis
We are the warriors of
real courage.

We design our battle
to liberate ourself.

We are mildly marching,
watching the wild
crisis ahead.

Few organs of our nation are
unhealthy due to unhygienic
sanitation.

We are trying to synchronise
the music of organs
to synthesise the symphony
of `oneness'.

*This was written and presented in the Poetry
Recitation Congregation (1995), Jawaharlal Nehru
University, New Delhi by the author.

EMOTIONS

Do not flick through
the catalogue of
my emotions.

Do not be a witness
to the naked parade
of my sentiments.

Do not go through
the alphabet
of my feelings.

Do not see the
amputated
numbed feelings
of despair.

Do not try to
converse with the
warmth of the gallows,
where my
Feelings and emotions
for you
fades...

MOMENTS

Never had I
Concluded my conversation
With you

Nor had I
Shrugged off the
Moments of love
I shared with you

Nor had I
Deciphered the reasons
for the demise of love..

Nor had I
bid adieu to
the warmth of
memory that sustains
the moments...of Love...

TSUNAMI-AN UNTOLD TRAGEDY

Life
ashored
is dead.

A few minutes
of your life
on the shores had
washed away
all our lives.

Orphaned thousands
and burdened
the future
with the episodes
of untold sorrows.

A costly lesson
to know the
other side of the
Beauty and Serenity
of the **SEA**.

`You had
Silently swallowed
all our
Peace and Happiness
-The only savings
of our life.